The Impact of New Technology on the International Media Foreign Policy

Nicholas Hopkinson

March 1995

Wilton Park Paper 97

Report based on Wilton Park Conference 427: The Media and International Affairs: International Crises, New Communication Technologies, and Their Effect On Public Consciousness (28 November–2 December 1995).

London: HMSO

© Crown copyright 1995
Applications for reproduction should be made to HMSO
Copyright Unit
ISBN 0 11 701929 1
ISSN 0953–6542

Published by HMSO and available from:

HMSO Publications Centre
(Mail, fax and telephone orders only)
PO Box 276, London SW8 5DT
Telephone orders 0171 873 9090
General enquiries 0171 873 0011
(queuing system in operation for both numbers)
Fax orders 0171 873 8200

HMSO Bookshops
49 High Holborn, London WC1V 6HB
(counter service only)
0171 873 0011 Fax 0171 831 1326
68–69 Bull Street, Birmingham B4 6AD
0121 236 9696 Fax 0121 236 9699
33 Wine Street, Bristol BS1 2BQ
0117 9264306 Fax 0117 9294515
9–21 Princess Street, Manchester M60 8AS
0161 834 7201 Fax 0161 833 0634
16 Arthur Street, Belfast BT1 4GD
01232 238451 Fax 01232 235401
71 Lothian Road, Edinburgh EH3 9AZ
0131 228 4181 Fax 0131 229 2734
The HMSO Oriel Bookshop
The Friary, Cardiff CF1 4AA
01222 395548 Fax 01222 384347

HMSO's Accredited Agents
(see Yellow Pages)

and through good booksellers

Contents

		page
1	Introduction	1
2	The Increasing Use of the Internet	2
3	New Broadcast Technologies	4
4	The Influence of the Media and Public Opinion on Foreign Policy	7
5	The Media and Humanitarian Agencies	9
6	Case Studies of Coverage of Crises and Media Influence on Western Policy	10
	Ethiopia	11
	Afghanistan	11
	The Gulf War	12
	Somalia	12
	Former Yugoslavia	13
	Rwanda	15
7	Technology and the Media in Emerging Democracies	15
	The Commonwealth	16
	The Middle East	18
	Central Europe	20
8	Conclusions	21
	List of Participants	24

1 Introduction

The globalisation of the media is being driven by the rapid development of new technologies, corporate debt, and revenue enhancement. Media conglomerates are expanding rapidly into foreign markets because this is where revenue growth is fastest. The domination of the global media by a few Anglo-Saxon conglomerates, closely identified with a few magnates, is largely attributable to the fact that they acquired the commercial power first and that they were also first to adopt new technologies. But ultimately it is the banks, rather than the shareholders, that are driving ferocious competition and 'mergermania' undertaken by conglomerates such as Bertelsmann AG, Capital Cities-ABC, News Corporation, Pearson, Sony, Thomson, Time Warner, Turner Broadcasting, and Viacom-Paramount. Thus, for many the 'information superhighway' is largely a story of mergers, acquisitions, and "a variety of strategic economic alliances between and among different communication industry entities, including computer, cable, broadcasting, telephony, publishing and various on-line data services".[1]

The 'information superhighway' is "made possible by digitalisation and fibre optics that connect the telephone, the television and the computer, creating an interactive media system with extensive reach".[2] Telephone, computer and television are converging, thus all becoming the same device. For example, telephone messages can be received on computer. Popular television programmes can be received in seven different ways including by telephone and on-line. However, cost factors, consumer demand and access do not appear to have been considered: "While technological possibilities may be infinite and while the market may produce thousands of choices, where only a relatively few are available

---

[1] Everette E. Dennis, *Mapping and Understanding the Information Superhighway*, speech presented at the international forum on 'The Global Networking Society', University of Madrid, 9–11 May 1994, p 3.
[2] Dennis, E., *ibid.*, p. 5.

today, that does not mean that there is a viable audience for what is likely to be made available".[3]

This paper examines how the new technologies are changing the nature of news broadcasting and, in turn, influencing foreign policy decision-making.[4] It also examines how international humanitarian agencies are using new technology, and how new technology is enabling media conglomerates to expand into emerging markets, a subject that involves the examination of telecommunications infrastructures and the freedom of the media in emerging democracies.

2 The Increasing Use of the Internet[5]

The Internet is a global network of computers connected through broadband, fibre-optic telephone lines that quickly transmit huge amounts of digital data. As of July 1994, the Internet had grown to a total of 3.2 million 'host' computers, 63 per cent of which were located in the US, allowing 20 to 30 million people worldwide to have access.

About 30 international humanitarian and human rights organisations are currently using the Internet on a regular basis. Internet capabilities, specifically, electronic mail (E-mail), electronic conferencing and bulletin boards, are primarily being used to facilitate inter and intra-organisational communication including co-ordinating activities across organisations and across different branches of the same organisation; cross-checking information on

---

[3] Dennis, E., *ibid.*, p. 3–4.
[4] see N. Hopkinson, *The Media and International Affairs After the Cold War*, Wilton Park Paper 74, HMSO, London, 1993.
[5] this section draws considerably on the Freedom Forum Research Group, *Communicators of Conscience: How Humanitarian and Human Rights Organisations Are Tapping Into the Internet*, Special (Preliminary) Report, The Freedom Forum Media Studies Center, Columbia University, New York, 1994, pps. 5 and 20.

human rights abuses from different organisational sources, and communicating with field workers. The Internet is also being used as a depository for breaking news from trouble spots around the world. Archival information is being added to the Internet daily including electronic newsletters; research reports on relief efforts; disaster situation reports; descriptive information about agencies and programmes; directories of organisations; and background information on international humanitarian law.

Humanitarian agencies acknowledge that the Internet has 'enormous potential' to assist them take quick action in emergency situations and co-ordinating relief operations during disasters. When a disaster unfolds, there is a critical need for humanitarian groups to obtain information that would allow them to gauge how safe conditions are for relief workers, locations of food stockpiles and the state of the country's economic infrastructure. Use of the Internet may allow aid groups to get such information far more quickly and, using it when they arrive, to avoid duplicating efforts and competing for scarce resources within the country. Discussions are underway for a joint initiative between the UN Department of Humanitarian Affairs (DHA) and the US State Department called 'ReliefNet', a project aimed at using the Internet as a coordination vehicle for planning early relief efforts around pending crises.

The Internet makes the interception or censorship of messages virtually impossible, and helps disseminate information to the general public, thus cutting down on mailing costs, processing time, and production costs. The declining costs of computer technology and the infrastructure needed mean that Internet could become widely available even to resource-poor organisations in the near future.

However, there are constraints limiting the use of the Internet. Accessing much of the information requires a great deal of user sophistication. In many parts of the world, computer illiteracy co-incides with basic illiteracy. Accordingly, Internet penetration in much of the developing world will be severely limited for some time to come. Even though children are often less afraid of using new technology than their parents, traditional forms of communication such as mail, phone calls, and faxes are likely to be heavily used for some time.

Another problem is that much misinformation can be easily fed into the Internet. Increasingly it is unclear whether the information on the Internet is true. For example, pictures can be electronically altered – only $10,000 is needed to create an entirely synthetic news event. If images no longer tell the truth, they must be labelled lest people, or even policy-makers, draw the wrong conclusions. One implication is that journalists are still needed on location to confirm stories.

3 New Broadcast Technologies

Originally television news was presented by a reader off-screen, rather like radio news. There has since been a shift towards the journalist as editor and producer, and from the newsroom to on-location. With the introduction of computers, journalists can access all the news all of the time as well as access sources and archives more rapidly. The newsroom's ability to respond swiftly to events in a comprehensive way is improved. The editor can make changes on screen, enabling change at the last minute. With fewer deadlines, journalists can go 'on air' without a finished product.

The new revolution in electronic broadcasting is founded upon "computers that are more powerful, faster and more reliable, yet smaller and cheaper; tumbling unit costs for on-line data storage; new data compression techniques; improved communications technology; advanced computer applications which combine astonishing functionality with ease of use.

Tape-based technology is under threat as broadcasters adopt digital techniques, where images and sound are stored as digital data on computer hard disks rather than as analogue data on tape. Many radio broadcasters are now routinely using digital audio systems . . . (Although) the average desktop personal computer (can) store several hours of digital audio, it (can)not manage more than a few seconds of broadcast-quality video. Part of the solution is video compression, which uses complicated mathematical techniques to reduce the amount of space required . . . unlike tape-based systems, (digital editing systems) are essentially non-linear and allow random access to video and audio which can be non-destructively edited and re-edited, with new material capable of being dropped into the middle of already edited packages. This (corrects) the retrograde step introduced by video-tape which, unlike film, cannot be physically cut and stuck together. With Non-linear editing, video chips can be added electronically.

For most broadcasters, however, the availability of digital editing alone is not enough to prompt them into a wholesale move away from videotape. Several more elements are required, of which the first is Digital News Gathering. Today, images are still recorded onto tape and must then be encoded before digital editing is possible. This can be an unacceptably lengthy process . . . What is required, and what the industry is racing to deliver, is an economic way of recording images directly onto hard disk in an already-compressed format, bypassing tape and allowing immediate access for editing.

Another technological challenge concerns the speed with which digital images can be sent from one place to another . . . it takes up proportionately large amounts of bandwidth when sent across networks and through communications channels. Compression is again part of the solution, along with the development of new networking standards such as Asychronous Transfer Mode (ATM) which can transmit data over 15 times as fast as ordinary Ethernet . . . (when) full-blown video networks where central servers with massive storage capability are accessed by multiple concurrent recording, editing and playback systems (are) packaged into products which are both reliable and cost-efficient, the revolution will really be upon us . . .

The next major challenge is to integrate this emerging digital video and audio production capability with editorial and management functions . . . The aim is to build a broadcast computer infrastructure which will allow a single person at a single workstation to access and process all of the data and material necessary to put together a broadcast video, audio, still images, graphics and text. Other functions will include graphics, archiving, resource management, accounting functions . . . Before too long (there may be) an increasing exportation of production capability into the field, with reporters using laptop PCs not only to communicate with base but to edit pictures, dub audio and create graphics and titles, then filing back a concise finished product rather than voluminous raw material".[6]

The new technology opens up the possibility of considerable savings for media conglomerates. Television crews now comprise two individuals instead of five. In newsrooms, there is now a single control. Improvements in the storage of information makes news gathering more efficient. The recycling of material for re-broadcast and moving away from news bulletins at set times of the day presents opportunities for savings in rolling news. As the costs of new technology and production plunge, barriers to entry for new players become lower. Nevertheless, many firms are still deterred from introducing new technology because they believe they are unable to make a quick profit.

Another barrier to introducing new technology is deregulation: "(in the US, for example) different sectors of the information infrastructure offer legislators and regulators different (problems) . . . (in the) print media, access is not an issue, since printing presses are readily available and newspapers are inexpensive. The First Amendment is all the regulation that that sector requires. For the telephone, content is private, and thus not subject to regulation. The regulatory issue is the conduit, the actual wires, which law requires be made available to consumers . . . access and availability are not a problem for the consumer, since anyone with a radio or television has access to the airwaves and broadcast reception is free. Regulation comes at the broadcaster's end: the

---

[6] Adrian Scott, *Leaping into a New World*, COMBROAD, Commonwealth Broadcasting Association, Issue number 106, March 1995, pps. 4–5.

broadcast spectrum is regulated, as is broadcast content . . . cable (like programming content) is the most regulated".[7]

Light weight and easy to use cameras, such as Hi-8s, and high-powered satellite technology have made far more real-time war coverage possible than ever before. Ironically, an inverse relationship has developed between the wealth of recorded coverage and how much is actually transmitted. The new technologies will reduce the media's old role as 'gatekeeper' – increasingly the journalist will be more of a travel guide through the 'information glut'.

4 The Influence of the Media and Public Opinion on Foreign Policy

If there are no television images, then there is no serious coverage of a crisis. However, if there are images, governments are forced to react. The new technology adds true immediacy to crises. Because it is not yesterday's news, the public realise that their opinion can affect policy-making. By highlighting policy dilemmas, real-time images can put pressure on policy makers to make choices and to decide priorities in a compressed response time. Fearing that a powerful media story can mobilise a strong public opinion overnight, politicians are obliged to make vague and bland statements.

Foreign policy is more influenced by public opinion than in the past. It is no longer solely decided behind tightly closed doors because interest groups have become more organised, and because the media, particularly the electronic media, have essentially become a surrogate for public opinion. However, public opinion still does not widely determine foreign policy. Foreign policy

---

[7] The Freedom Forum Media Studies Center Research Group, *Separating Fact from Fiction on the Information Superhighway*, Freedom Forum Media Studies Center, Columbia University, New York, p. 27.

issues are rarely in the top two or three major issues concerning the public. Public opinion has few means to express itself coherently and systematically, and it will thus usually follow leaders. Campaigns using letters, telephone calls, faxes, political contacts and the media, and in some cases street protests, are usually not enough. Even if inflamed, the strength of the public's arguments is generally shallow and its impact temporary.

Srebrenica, the Ahmici massacre, the Sarajevo Market massacre, or the dead US Ranger being dragged through the streets of Mogadishu may be apparent recent examples of how television forced changes in policy. However, the new orthodoxy is that television informs but it does not influence as much as once believed. The media highlights policy problems but it fails to solve them; it shapes the policy agenda but does not dictate responses. Television's ability to provide contemporaneous video must not be confused with a power to drive policy-making.

Most government responses are short-term damage limitation exercises which are cost effective and are aimed at gaining the maximum public approval. Governments aim to be seen to react without undermining the ongoing specific policy focus. Reacting can be anything from a UN Resolution to sending out a press spokesman. Governments may express concern, or outrage, or issue a statement of condemnation, and even announce a modest humanitarian commitment of supplies: "organis(ing) a relief effort is a highly visible, reactive response. But it is not a change in foreign policy – it is a diplomatic and public palliative. Governments give the impression of full engagement but the reality is inaction: if television images had the influence on policy that many assume, there would have been a pre-emptive or preventive policy response to Rwanda".[8]

Politicians and officials, perhaps naturally, deny that news coverage has a real impact on policy decisions. They can regard television as trite, crude and incomplete. Television plays too

---

[8] Nik Gowing, *International Herald Tribune*, 1 August 1994.

much to the heart, and not enough to the head. Governments have to follow a rational pre-determined policy. Real-time television coverage of humanitarian conflicts will create emotions, but ultimately make no difference to the fundamental calculations of diplomats and officials who are used to working methodically, slowly, and reflectively. Very few European ministers ever have the time or inclination to watch television news. If they do, it is because an incident has been brought to their attention by anguished staff or family members. However, if a government is weak and does not have clear, predetermined policies, then the media will have greater influence.

5 The Media and Humanitarian Agencies

If the media do not have the impact on foreign policy makers, donors and the public as once believed, then the job of humanitarian organisations will become more difficult. Humanitarian agencies and the media have developed a common interest. Without the media, refugees would not be on the international agenda; equally journalists would not have such dramatic stories.

The recent history of the United Nations High Commissioner for Refugees (UNHCR) is illustrative. In 1989, the UNHCR decided that if it was to be able to protect the world's refugees, if it was to get the broader refugee issue on the international agenda, it would have to adopt a policy of transparency and mobilise public opinion through the media. With racism and xenophobia on the rise in the 1980s and 1990s, Western politicians were not eager to promote pro-refugee positions or to push through legislation on humanitarian aid. Without the funds to buy television advertising, the UNHCR consciously forged a closer relationship with the news media in order to tap large sums of money from governments and individuals.

The UNHCR knew that it would not be able to convince the media by lying about failures or stonewalling queries. Humanitarian agencies have to be upfront and credible. Although many failures have been highlighted, the strategy of greater transparency has worked. Discounting 'compassion fatigue', public opinion is energised by suffering – when the public wants action, governments scramble to be the first on the scene. Humanitarian agencies therefore believe that television coverage has forced politicians to act.

As television editors remain reluctant to accept unconfirmed video stories from humanitarian agencies warning of impending disasters, the media acts as a 'late warning system'. For example, during the Rwandan crisis, it took weeks to get pledges of help from governments and another week before help arrived at Goma. However, it would have taken months if it had not been for the appalling television images.

6 Case Studies of Coverage of Crises and Media Influence on Western Policy

Media coverage of humanitarian crises is decided in a rather arbitrary manner. Decisions involve a wide range of factors including ease of access, the safety of camera crews, newsworthiness, cost, quality of coverage, and a judgement as to whether viewers and governments will be concerned by the wider political and strategic implications of the crisis. Sometimes the cameras have been on location, but the programme editors never felt moved enough to transmit the images. Thus many crises, such as Abkhazia, Angola, Liberia, Sudan and Tajikistan have hardly been, or have never been, broadcast on Western television. However, Somalia and Rwanda are exceptions because the massive scale of the horror was so powerful that it overrode the apparent absence of Western strategic interests. Thus while satellite dishes made Sarajevo a visible global symbol of Serb agression, the even greater horrors of the Croat siege of Mostar and elsewhere in the former Yugoslavia were rarely filmed. However, Gorazde did attract world attention despite the absence of cameras.

The following brief case studies show that the new view of the marginal influence of the media appears to founded largely on a few post-Cold War cases, in particular the complex crisis in the former Yugoslavia. They illustrate that the media's influence on policy varies case by case.

Ethiopia

During the Ethiopian famine of 1984, initially the government did not allow the press anywhere near the scene. There were no pictures and, as a result, there was little aid. Everyone, including the governments with embassies in Addis Ababa, knew something terrible was happening and they probably were aware of the full extent of the horror. It was not until Mohammed Amin, a cameraman for Visnews, and Michael Buerk of the BBC reached the famine area that the first pictures appeared. It was only then that help began to be offered. Viewers around the world literally beseiged their governments and forced them into action.

Afghanistan

The current lack of interest in Afghanistan is attributable to the fact that the conflict has been underway for more than 15 years and that a big power is no longer actively involved. With the end of the Cold War, the major donor nations no longer have a strategic interest in such a faraway squabble with no obvious solution in sight. There is also the problem of access.

The intense media interest during the 1980s contrasts markedly with the situation today with only BBC radio and a couple of wire services maintaining a presence. In 1994, there was never more than one television crew in Kabul, a city that has seen much more destruction and suffering than Sarajevo. Without pictures, and thus an indignant public demanding action, governments see little political capital in a major humanitarian intervention in Central Asia.

The Gulf War

Television images are widely believed to have ended both the Vietnam and Gulf Wars. Images of carnage from the Mutla Gap 'Highway of Death' are believed to have contributed to President Bush's decision to 'cut short' the war. Partly, the decision was made after 99 hours of war for purely symbolic reasons. Although the Bush Administration was alarmed by the Mutla Gap images, in retrospect, it appears that President Bush may have acted under a misperception. He probably thought back to Vietnam and believed, arguably wrongly, that television images of carnage would turn Americans against the war. However, American audiences were less affected by the sight of Iraqi, as opposed to American, casualties.

Somalia

Since the Gulf War, there has been a new generation of armed conflicts. Somalia is cited as an example of a crisis that gained wide coverage, but much too late. The fighting in Somalia began in early 1991 with the onset of drought and the creation of hundreds of thousands of refugees. The cameras were not present and the humanitarian response was apathetic. The world only began to take an interest in December 1991 when an NGO report from inside Somalia told of hundreds of children dying each day of starvation.

All UN agencies share the blame for not succeeding in focusing world attention on the tragedy, partly because all their humanitarian efforts were basically unsuccessful. If it had not been for the graphic images coming out of Somalia, that crisis could have gone the way of similar crises in Angola and the Sudan which are virtually unknown to the general public, and are therefore not seen as a priority by governments.

The notorious images of the dead US soldier being dragged though the streets of Mogadishu is popularly credited with having led to the US decision to withdraw. However, President Clinton did not announce the troop withdrawal because he was personally revolted by the images. National Security Adviser, Tony Lake, claimed that he never saw the pictures of a dozen dead Americans. The Clinton Administration responded because of the torrent of phone calls to Congress demanding action. Foreign policy was therefore shaped by public opinion. However, another interpretation argues that the decision to end US commitment in Somalia was taken before the images appeared. This gives rise to the view that policymakers may use emotive images, or the presumed public response to them, to rationalise policy decisions (in this case to curtail involvement) already taken.

Former Yugoslavia

There is also disagreement over the media's influence on Western policy-making in the crisis in the former Yugoslavia. The majority view is that television has not had a positive, constructive influence on foreign policy. Governments have used the media to avoid responsibility and to delay difficult decisions. Delay has made the crisis much worse. However, television may have had some influence by exposing absurd inconsistencies which policy-makers were unaware of or had not thought through, thus forcing policy in new directions.

To a significant degree, cause has been confused with effect. Instead of seeing a difficult crisis 'causing' Western inaction, it is far more accurate to see a collapse of Western security institutions 'causing' the crisis to emerge in the first place. At each step along the trail, the Serbs, as well as the Croats and Muslims, had to ask themselves, will the West stop me if I cross this line? One or two lines held firm but most did not. The Western institutional response was completely incoherent, and it remains so.

Thus the real story of the whole conflict is that international security institutions no longer function in the Post-Cold War World. Most of the media has avoided driving home the very tough questions of why these institutions have failed to deal with the crisis. From the beginning of the crisis, the West preferred a humanitarian response because it was not willing to do anything else. American policy-makers realised that if efforts were cast in terms of aid, then the West would get off the hook for finding an end to the war. The UN picked up humanitarian aid as a *raison d'etre* for its presence in Bosnia. The UN aid convoys saved an unquantifiable number of lives and created humanitarian ghettos. But many now argue, including the UN, that the aid in response to television images probably prolonged the war.

In the early stages of the war, the pictures of Serb shelling of Dubrovnic and Vukovar did not affect policy. Although ITN's shocking August 1992 pictures of Muslim men in Serb concentration camps did help close many camps, the Sarajevo market massacre of 68 people, an apparent example of the impact of television images, did not influence policy. There was some media speculation that since the massacre took place while President Clinton was in Japan, it had an unusual effect on him because, being jet-lagged, he had spent a lot of extra time watching the gruesome pictures on CNN. CNN subsequently declared several times in news reports that its coverage had changed the policy. However, the massacre, not the images, catalysed a diplomatic process that had been underway for weeks. Europe, led by France, told the US that they could no longer put up with fruitless negotiations in Geneva while risking the lives of their troops on the ground. Weeks before the marketplace massacre a whole new set of policy instruments was coming together, based around the European idea of limited force to bring about a settlement on Western terms. The massacre was certainly a catalyst, but it did not produce the new policy. Policy would have changed anyway, albeit more slowly, without the massacre. Thus throughout the conflict, declarations of horror or condemnation were usually mis-read in the media as signals of a hardening of policy. They were 'pseudo decisions for pseudo action'.

In a civil war situation, balanced reporting is difficult but it is achievable. In Bosnia and Rwanda, it was not a case of the good versus the bad, but the better guys versus the worse guys. For example, the Ahmici massacre instigated by the Muslims complicated the picture of the Bosnia-Herzegovina crisis and made it easier for NATO to reject air strikes. The image of the Muslims as the guilty party was soon forgotten, and the Serbs quickly regained their position as sole evil party in the war. In many cases, there can be no doubt who is the more culpable and the most innocent. A story about Serb atrocities does not always have to be balanced by a story of Bosnian or Croat atrocities. It is a case that one ethnic group has committed many more atrocities than others. The West has been taken in by the Serbian characterisation of the war as an ethnic civil war; the Western response would have been different if was initially treated as a struggle between fascists and democrats.

Rwanda

Rwanda took place at a time of military down-sizing and concern with events closer to home: "because of commitments to Bosnia, the bigger European nations effectively turned a blind eye to Rwanda".[9] A pilot camera crew was sent to Rwanda a few months before the crisis, but the images did not portray a crisis. The public heard about the crisis in Rwanda, and saw it intermittently on television, but not night-after-night as in the case of Sarajevo. While all major networks maintained staff in Sarajevo, Zagreb and Belgrade, for the first three months of the Rwanda crisis no satellite dish was on location because of the dangers and the initial physical difficulty of getting to the scenes of slaughter. The images of carnage and the despatch of the 5,500 man UN force, were far too little, too late. In spite of warning signals eight weeks before the Goma cholera catastrophe on the Tanzanian border, humanitarian aid only came with the images of widespread death.

7 Technology and the Media in Emerging Democracies

Improved communications technology, whether used within or across borders, combined with political and economic reform, is changing the nature of the media and societies in emerging democracies.

---

[9] Gowing, N., *ibid.*

The Commonwealth

Democracy must be nurtured by strengthening the media. It is hoped that the Commonwealth Heads of Government Meeting at Auckland in 1995 will be able to include in their communiqué, or in a separate statement, a declaration that freedom of expression is a clear Commonwealth principle. Belief in a free and independent media is not mentioned in the 1971 Declaration of Commonwealth Principles nor in the 1991 Harare Declaration, a fact that reflects badly on the Commonwealth. If the absence of free and diverse media in many parts of the Commonwealth were taken up, as the evils of apartheid were tackled, diplomatic and other pressures could turn out to be suprisingly effective.

In many of the emerging democracies of the Commonwealth, there is a total shortage of the new media. At Independence, many Commonwealth countries, adopted what was in the 1940s and 1950s, the British pattern for broadcasting, namely a monopoly corporation modelled on the BBC. But while Britain has developed an electronic media of great diversity, many African, Pacific and Asian countries have imposed greater government control over their monopoly electronic media, even though their press, in many cases, is very free. Such countries use various arguments in defence of such arrangements. They argue that the monopoly public service broadcaster is used to educate and uplift. There is no 'sleaze' or pornography, and there are many programmes on improving agriculture, health, education, hygiene, and family planning. More controversially, countries like Kenya argue the need for the Kenya Broadcasting Corporation to aid 'Nation-Building'. For other countries, radio is essential as a means for national development and decentralised education in the South Pacific where many outlying islands do not have electricity. Monopoly broadcasters also favour the status quo because their monopoly allows them to earn income from advertising, something that would be quickly lost to the commercial sector if there were deregulation.

Change in ownership is, however, begining to happen quickly in some countries while in others, not at all. The greatest example of the pressures for diversity is India where there is a free press, but monopoly television in Doordarshan, and monopoly radio, All India Radio, both of which earn revenue from advertising. These two broadcasting organisations had a mission to inform and uplift, to maintain family values and to build a united nation out of linguistic and ethnic diversity. However, there is universal acknowledgement that the news is slow and prone either to guidance or self-censorship. For example, it took several hours before clearance could be obtained to broadcast the news of the assassination of Prime Minister Mrs. Indira Ghandi. Even her son, Rajiv, had to tune to the BBC World Service to find out what had happened.

But suddenly STAR Television started beaming Western entertainment programmes, and news from BBC World Service Television (WST) and CNN arrived. The familiar constraints of monopoly broadcasting no longer held. The Asian Broadcaster, secure all these years in his own territory with a monopoly on the airwaves, content with 'mild' programming, has inevitably been shocked out of complacency. The captive audiences no longer exist; the importunate advertiser has suddenly become very cool. Audiences and revenues are beginning to slip away. Accordingly, Indian broadcasting has now been restructured, and added Doordarshan 2, the former metropolitan channel with some material from independent producers, and Doordarshan 3, an upmarket channel for opinion formers. In addition, there are licensed new satellite operators such as JAIN TV and TV1 due to be launched in March 1995. Doordarshan International has also been developed as an international television satellite operation which will serve expatriate Indians and others who enjoy watching Indian programmes. While India has still retained control of its domestic broadcasting, it has changed radically within the past three years. It now has outlets for independents within the national broadcasting organisations, and the changes are unlikely to stop there.

The situation in most of Africa is quite different. Satellite television has not yet affected Africa to anything like the extent it has impacted on Asia. BBC WST, CNN and MTV are only available on cable, not free-to-air as in India. This is because the puchasing power, growing so fast in Asia that it is able to justify commercial advertising rates on STAR TV, does not exist in most of Africa; channels have to be sustained through the payment mechanisms of cable. Deregulation is likely to come first in radio. However, there are countries where private broadcasting and a free press are not on the agenda. Nigeria, for example, still has state broadcasting. It used to have a free press. However, in June 1994 the illegal regime closed down two newspaper houses including the leading liberal daily newspaper, *The Guardian*. Opposition lawyers, politicians, and journalists are now barred from leaving the country. The decline of the economy and the high costs of newsprint are beginning to affect the impact of the vigorous pro-democracy media. If there is no improvement in the economy, many newspapers and magazines will disappear from the newsstands and General Sani Abacha will achieve his goal of a nation 'without newspapers'.

The Middle East

Only three years ago there were only one or two national television channels in each Middle Eastern country. Today plans and investments have been made, and technology has been developed to launch up to 18 new channels. These new channels, to be broadcast from satellites to paying individuals across the Arab world, will be in addition to the nine Arabic channels that are already available to the owners of satellite receiver dishes. Of these, the Middle East Broadcasting Centre (MEBC) is the only independent pan-Arab channel broadcast domestically and also on satellite. In the next five to 10 years, high power digital television signals will be available over the Gulf, and thereafter the rest of the Middle East.

The issues of disruption of cultures, intrusion into domestic politics, incursion on national sovereignty, or at the very least what is the appropriate regulation of this media newcomer, are live and acute. It is clear that in every part of the world, governments and legislators have not anticipated the revolutionary growth of foreign television. For example, CNN, previously unheard of in the Arabic world, now has a wider audience than national programmes. The future has arrived so fast that governments did not have time to plan for it.

Government in all countries are quickly realising the dangers as well as the benefits of trans-frontier broadcasting. Television programmes can influence and change people and their values. Sometimes this is beneficial, where new and enriching information is shown, but very often foreign programmes show the worst of what is happening in other countries and contain items that offend those whose culture and values were not considered when the programme was made.

It is the responsibility of governments to protect their own society and their own national and religious culture from unacceptable television programmes that, for the first time, are available from satellites orbiting over their countries. What is acceptable and what is not acceptable will always be debated but it is increasingly recognised that these decisions have to be made and moral guidance made clear where physical prevention is difficult. Where satellite television channels broadcast programmes that are not acceptable, even on payment of a subscription, clear guidance is necessary and an alternative choice of television channels made available to satisfy the appetite for more variety.

For example, in Europe, most countries now ban unacceptable pornography channels delivered by satellite. There is a strict rule in Europe that there must be a set percentage of programmes produced in the EU, the object of which is both to preserve national production of programmes and, more importantly, to protect national cultures from excessive foreign programming. Turner Broadcasting has already discovered that they cannot simply export whole programme channels from the US to Europe.

With the increase in the number of channels, there must be some control over what is shown. This is particularly necessary in the Arab Muslim world, as it is going to be even more difficult to protect Arab and Islamic culture from foreign influence than it is to protect European culture, that has already been substantially influenced by foreign programmes.

The introduction of re-broadcasting of satellite channels terrestrially either by free-over-air or controlled multi-channel multi-point distribution systems (MMDS) is the most obvious and efficient way to ensure that viewers both have a choice of channels and that these channels are acceptable. The Direct Broadcast Satellite (DBS) channels then become unnecessary and can be controlled by making them illegal and preventing the sale by subscription. Pirate radio and television channels have been controlled in this way in the United Kingdom where it is illegal to subscribe to, or advertise on, such channels. By having a subscription MMDS system in each country, the revenue from subscriptions to the channels remains in the country, rather than being paid outside the country to the DBS operator.

Central Europe

New technology, political reform, privatisation and deregulation have encouraged a rapid democratisation of the media in Central and Eastern Europe. There is now a proliferation in the number of publications and television channels. For example, Hungarians can tune to 26 television channels and 10 Hungarian cities have more than three daily newspapers (by contrast only 10 US cities have more than one daily newspaper).

From 1957 to the 1980s, Communist governments wanted to stop people from tuning into Western broadcasting. When controls were relaxed, satellite dishes were imported from the West, and satellite signals were fed into existing master antenna systems. Telephone installers, television repair people, and government telephone workers, rapidly entered the cable business. The tremendous appetite for uncensored foreign language programming immediately after the fall of Communism has waned. Now national programming is strongly preferred, giving rise to local production companies, or at least local dubbing or subtitling firms.

While governments in the Czech Republic, Hungary, Poland and Slovakia have been engaged in often heated internal debate over control of public radio and television broadcasting, cable network operators have been quietly wiring up quickly. Between a fifth and a third of homes are receiving multi-channel satellite programming, half of which are served by commercial cable operators with the remainder by DBS. Cable television growth has outrun government interest in the industry and attempts to regulate it. Many laws affecting cable franchises, copyrights, technical requirements and broadcast licensing are still being written, or interpreted, or have yet to be enforced. Many systems operate in ignorance of and often in conflict with the law. For example, it is rare to find a cable operator paying for any programming captured from a satellite.

Foreign investment has helped establish the largest cable networks in each country, but most systems are locally owned. Most commercial cable operators carry all available terrestrial and satellite local language programming but they have not yet developed an interest in using the power of their networks to inform viewers or to shape public opinion. While many of the networks remain primitive, some are state of the art, built on fibre-optic grids with broadband channel and back-channel capability with the latest equipment. A few have recognised their potential as programme, telephone and interactive data providers and are working to gain a foothold in those areas. Given the great need to expand and modernise telephone systems and digital communication, it is likely that telephone, data and video services are going to converge in cable systems very quickly in Central Europe.

8 Conclusions

1. Corporate debt, earnings growth and new technology are driving globalisation of the media.

2. The world will increasingly divide into a world of technology haves and have-nots. The new broadcast revolution itself is founded upon computers that are more powerful, faster, more

reliable, smaller and cheaper; tumbling unit costs; new data compression techniques; improved communications technologies; and advanced computer applications which combine functionality with ease of use.

3. Most of Europe is around two years behind North America in the use of the latest broadcast technology and the Internet. Opinion varies between North Americans and many Europeans as to how much the Internet will change the work of governments and the media. Already humanitarian organisations are using the Internet to improve co-ordination of operations. Some believe that for the Internet to have a significant impact, individuals and organisations need access, money and time. Varying levels of literacy, technology and connectivity mean that traditional forms of communication such as mail, phone calls, and faxes are likely to be heavily used for some time yet.

4. The new technology will reduce the media's old role as 'gatekeeper'. Increasingly journalists will act as facilitators and travel guides through the 'information superhighway'.

5. The new technology has created a rapid growth in the availability of images of humanitarian crises, the fuel that ignites public opinion. However, there is now an inverse relationship between the wealth of recorded coverage and how much is actually transmitted.

6. Television does not put pressure on policy-makers as much as once believed. It highlights policy problems but it fails to solve them. It shapes the policy agenda but does not dictate responses. Television's contemporaneous images must not be confused with a power to drive policy-making. However, this new orthodoxy may rely too heavily on the current complicated conflict in the former Yugoslavia and the natural reluctance of politicians and officials to admit to journalists, their keenest critics or even adversaries, that they influence their decisions. Reliance on a theory based on a few recent conflicts downplays the widely acknowledged vital role that the media played in ending the

Vietnam and Gulf Wars. Accordingly, it would appear that the impact of the media varies according to the case under consideration.

7. Humanitarian organisations hope that the new orthodoxy concerning the media's influence is wrong, but they suspect that it is right. If the influence of the media is not as great as was once believed, humanitarian agencies fear that their ability to promote their activities and raise funds will be adversely affected.

8. Foreign policy is more influenced by public opinion than in the past because interest groups have become more organised and because the modern media increasingly acts as a surrogate for public opinion. New technology adds true immediacy to international crises, thus giving publics the belief that they can influence events. Nevertheless, public opinion is often incoherent and therefore it will usually follow foreign policy opinion formers. Public opinion is more important if a government is weak.

9. It should not be forgotten that politicians and officials influence the media and public opinion. However, it is difficult for policy makers to use the media to influence public opinion in the desired direction.

10. The new technology is opening rapidly growing markets in the developing world and Central and Eastern Europe. New technology has made satellite and trans-frontier broadcasting possible, thus challenging national cultures, media monopolies, and restrictions on the media. In order to promote a free and pluralistic media, that is vital for democracy and good government, Western governments, firms and NGOs must help nurture a credible media, especially radio and print, in emerging democracies.

List of Participants

AALTONEN, Lauri: Ministry for Foreign Affairs, Helsinki
ALLEN, John: Royal Military Academy, Sandhurst
BACCHETTA, Gian-Battista: International Committee of the Red Cross, Geneva
BAKER, Kieran: Cable News International Inc, London
BENDITO, Alberto: Spanish Institute of International Affairs (CESEDEN), Madrid
BICKHAM, Edward: Hill and Knowlton (UK) Ltd; former Special Adviser to the Foreign Secretary, London
BRAYNE, Mark: BBC World Service, London
CARRUTHERS, Susie: University of Wales, Aberystwyth
CAWSON, Alan: University of Sussex, Falmer, Brighton
DENNIS, Everette: The Freedom Forum Media Studies Center, Columbia University, New York
EDERER, Markus: German Foreign Office, Bonn
EKSI, Oktay: *Hurriyet*, Istanbul; Turkish Press Council, Istanbul
FENTON, Tom: The Freedom Forum European Office, Zurich
FINDEISEN, Martina: Saxon Parliament, Dresden
FOA, Sylvana: UN High Commissioner for Refugees, Geneva
FOY, Colm: OECD Development Centre, Paris
FRIDNER, Peter: *Narodna Obroda*, Bratislava
GASSMANN, Pierre: International Committee of the Red Cross, Geneva
GAZSI, Shirley: Freedom Forum Media Studies Center, Columbia University, New York
GOWING, Nik: Channel Four News, London
HANDKE-LEPTIEN, Uta Ulrike: Treuhand Investigation Committee, Bonn
van den HEUVEL, Hans: Ministry of Defence, The Hague
HODGSON, Godfrey: Reuter Foundation Programme; University of Oxford
HOGE, Jim: *Foreign Affairs*, New York; Council on Foreign Relations, New York
HOPKINSON, Nicholas: Wilton Park, Steyning
HORVAT, Janos: Budapest Film and Television Office (MTV), Budapest
JOHANSSEN, Klaus-Peter: Deutsche Shell AG, Hamburg

KARKOUTI, Mustapha: Middle East Broadcasting Centre (MEBC), London
KENNEY, George: Consultant and Lecturer, Washington DC
KHASHABA, Hosny: *Asharq Al-Awsat*, London
KLAPPROTH, Stephan: Swiss Television, DRS, Zurich; Institute for Journalism, University of Freiburg
LANGHORNE, Richard: Wilton Park, Steyning
MacDONALD, Rich: C.S. First Boston, New York
MacVICAR, Sheila: ABC News Bureau, London
MÄKELÄ, Jarmo: Finnish Broadcasting Company, Helsinki
MARASH, David: ABC News, New York
MATANLE, Emma: Royal Institute of International Affairs, London
McGILL, Lawrence: The Freedom Forum Media Studies Center, Columbia University, New York
MEER, Christoph: Union of Mining and Energy, Sprockhoevel
MOELLER, Jens: TV2/Denmark, Odense
MÜCHLER, Günter: German Radio, Cologne
OTTOSEN, Rune: International Peace Research Institute (PRIO), Oslo
POCS, Balazs: *Nepczabadsaq*, Budapest
POWELL, Adam Clayton: The Freedom Forum Media Studies Center, Columbia University, New York
PRESTON, Alison: British Film Institute, London
RAMSDEN, Sir John: Foreign and Commonwealth Office, London
RENTSCHLER, James: Press Division, OECD, Paris
RIEF, Sylvia: Ministry for Economic Affairs, Vienna
ROZEMOND, Samuel: Netherlands Institue for International Relations, The Hague
SAVOLAINEN, Veli-Antti: CEO and Publisher, Helsinki
SCOTT, Adrian: Avid Technology, Langley, Berkshire
SCOTT, Colin: Brown University, Alexandria, Virginia
SHALNEV, Alexander: *Izvestia* Bureau, London
SIMOES, Rogério: *Folha de S. Paulo* Bureau, London
SMILLIE, Dirk: The Freedom Forum Media Studies Center, Columbia University, New York
SMITH, Elizabeth: Commonwealth Broadcasting Association, London
SOULEZ, Guillaume: Ministry of Foreign Affairs, Paris

SPASOVSKA, Verica: Deutsche Welle, Cologne
SPENCER, Claire: Wilton Park, Steyning
STEWART, Ian: Royal Military Academy, Sandhurst
STRZEMIECKI, Roman: *Wprost*, Warsaw
TIESSEN, Anita: Amnesty International, London
WALKER, Graham: BBC World Service Television, London
WALLACE, Jonathan: United Press International, London